B.C. —
Life is a 50p
Paperback

Johnny Hart

CORONET BOOKS
Hodder Fawcett, London

First published 1975 by Fawcett
Publications, Inc., New York

Coronet Edition 1977

Printed in Great Britain for Hodder Fawcett Ltd.,
Mill Road, Dunton Green, Sevenoaks, Kent (Editorial
Office: 47 Bedford Square, London, WC1 3DP) by
Hunt Barnard Printing Ltd.,
Aylesbury, Bucks. .

ISBN 0 340 21784 7

5·27

5·28

5.29

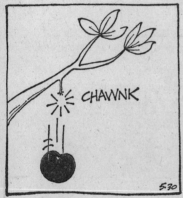

KISS
KISS
KISS
KISS
KISS

6·3

I HEAR SHE SNIFFS LAVA.

hart

6·4

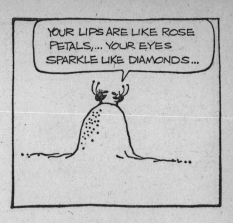

6-B

6.13

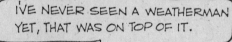

6·17

SHOOIE

7.1

7·2

YOUR BODY IS ANALOGOUS TO A BANK...YOU MAKE DEPOSITS BY EATING.

THE FOOD IS CONVERTED TO FAT AND STORED,...

THEN YOU MAKE WITHDRAWALS BY EXERCISING.

7·13

THE FIRST NATIONAL SHOULD HAVE YOUR RESERVES!

7·14

7.15

SHLUCK

DID I MAKE THE GREEN?

7·17

NO, BUT YOU GOT 20 YARDS ON YOUR TEE.

hart

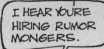

I HEAR YOU'RE HIRING RUMOR MONGERS.

THAT'S RIGHT, 10 CLAMS A DAY.

PETER'S PROPAGANDA SERVICE

7·21

...BUT THAT'S ONLY HALF WHAT YOU PAY THOR!

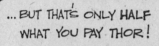

TRUE,...BUT WITH **HIM** IT'S A **JOB**.

PETER'S PROPAGANDA SERVICE

hart

7-28

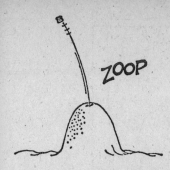

ZOOP

7·29

NAB

ONE OF THESE DAYS I'VE GOT TO FIX THAT TOASTER!

4

7:31

8-8

CRASH

8/10

ALL RIGHT, WHO LEFT THE STUFFED OWL IN THE DRIVEWAY?

ARE YOU CRAZY, JAKE? ..WE DON'T OWN A STUFFE....

MOTHERRR..

THAT'S THREE WALKS IN A ROW, KID.... YOU GETTIN' TIRED?

8·11

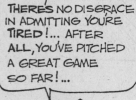

THERE'S NO DISGRACE IN ADMITTING YOU'RE TIRED!... AFTER ALL, YOU'VE PITCHED A GREAT GAME SO FAR!...

OK,.. I GUESS I AM BUSHED.

TAKE OVER FOR THE QUITTER.

8·13

5

8·19

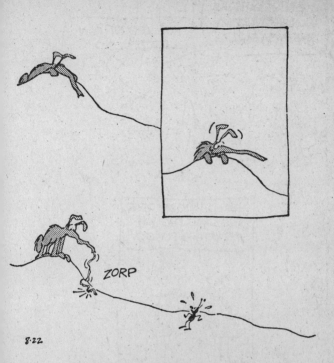

ZORP

8·22

WHAT ARE YOU STARING AT ?,
DIDNT YOUR TONGUE EVER
GO TO SLEEP BEFORE ?

hart

8-25

MEN, ... GREET THE NEWEST MEMBER OF OUR TEAM.

... I BOUGHT HIM FROM THE OPPOSITION.

9·27

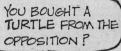

YOU BOUGHT A TURTLE FROM THE OPPOSITION?

I HAD TO!, ... HE HAD SIXTEEN STOLEN BASES AGAINST US.

8-21

9-2

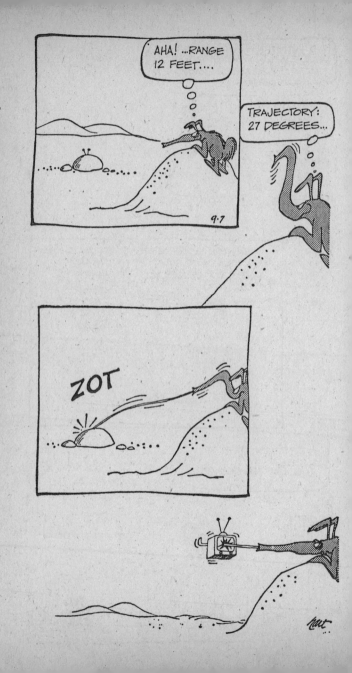

7.15

OK, GROG, LET'S SEE YOU SPLIT THE OL' UPRIGHTS!
COACH
9·17
COACH
PUNT
I SAID THE UPRIGHTS!

9·21

I WONDER IF MY STRENGTH IS REALLY IN MY HAIR.

WRONG AGAIN.

10-1

10·2

10.3

..THEREFORE, BY BREAKING IT DOWN TO ONE SINGLE FACTOR, WE CAN SAFELY CONCLUDE,

10·8

THAT THE ANSWER TO ALL OF THE WORLD'S PROBLEMS IS:

SCUDZO!... THE MOUTHWASH THAT REALLY SCROLLS YOUR NURD!

10·10

HOW MUCH TRUTH IS THERE, TO THE RUMOR: "CLAMS GOT LEGS." ?

TROGLODYTE

10·14

10.17

8

DO YOU EVER FIND YOURSELF, AT TIMES, WONDERING JUST WHO YOU ARE?

10·19

I GUESS SO, ...WHY DO YOU ASK?

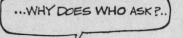

...WHY DOES WHO ASK?..

10-22

10-27

10-28

ZOT

SPLASH

10·30

I'VE NEVER SEEN ANYTHING SO PITIFUL IN MY WHOLE LIFE.

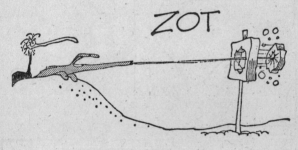

ZOT

11·4

B.C. ONE MORE TIME

All these books are available at your local bookshop or newsagent, or can be ordered direct from the publisher. Just tick the titles you want and fill in the form below.

Prices and availability subject to change without notice.

CORONET BOOKS, P.O. Box 11, Falmouth, Cornwall.

Please send cheque or postal order, and allow the following for postage and packing:

U.K. – One book 19p plus 9p per copy for each additional book ordered, up to a maximum of 73p.

B.F.P.O. and EIRE – 19p for the first book plus 9p per copy for the next 6 books, thereafter 3p per book.

OTHER OVERSEAS CUSTOMERS – 20p for the first book and 10p per copy for each additional book.

Name ....

Address ....

....